The Baby Ra

by

AND OTHER POEMS

Illustrated by Peter Viska

Melbourne
OXFORD UNIVERSITY PRESS
Oxford   Auckland

OXFORD UNIVERSITY PRESS

Oxford New York Toronto
Delhi Bombay Calcutta Madras Karachi
Kuala Lumpur Singapore Hong Kong Tokyo
Nairobi Dar es Salaam Cape Town
Melbourne Auckland
and associated companies in
Berlin Ibadan

OXFORD is a trademark of Oxford University Press

National Library of Australia
Cataloguing-in-Publication data:

Komninos.
    The baby rap and other poems.

    ISBN 0 19 553458 1.

    1. Children's poetry, Australian. I. Viska, Peter.
    II. Title.

A821.3

Typeset by Bookset, Melbourne
Printed by Impact Printing Pty Ltd, Victoria
Published by Oxford University Press,
253 Normanby Road, South Melbourne, Australia

Audiences young and old all around Australia have been enthralled by Komninos's mesmerising and hugely popular performances of his poetry. Komninos tours tirelessly, holding writing workshops for both adults and children, and performing everywhere from outback pubs to literary festivals. Komninos was born in Melbourne and now lives in Sydney with his wife and two children.

Peter Viska is a well-known animator and illustrator, mainly of children's books. Peter is a father of four, and describes himself as an iconoclastic optimist. His fans will agree that beneath the cheeky deftness of his drawings is a keen understanding of young people and their world.

Komninos and Peter had never met before *The Baby Rap*, but during the book's development discovered they are in fact third cousins! Thus *The Baby Rap* may be regarded as a true family collaboration.

The poems listed below are from the
Komninos collection first published in
1991 by the University of Queensland
Press, and are reproduced here with the
kind permission of the publisher.

the baby rap
in the city
granny's big pink underpants
household haiku
dripping taps
superwog

These poems are also available on the UQP
audio-cassette *Komninos*.

the baby rap

for maxim

well you hear a little grizzle
and you slowly unwrap
the bundle that is crying
in a heap on your lap
and you unwrap carefully
'cos it could be a trap
it wouldn't be the first time
he's had a mishap

the bundle could let loose
with a bum like a tap
that will spray you with poo
at the drop of a hat
splattering the mustard
on your clothes, on the mat
so you are ever so careful
how you unwrap

the shawl, the blanket
the sheets you unwrap
the nighties, the singlets
the nappies you unwrap
you unwrap, you unwrap
you unwrap, you unwrap

till he lies there naked
wearing nothing but a cap
do the baby rap, do the baby rap

and you get your cotton balls
and you clean up the crap
that has spread down his legs
round his front, up the back
every crease, every cranny
every crevice, every crack
and when he's all clean
you begin to wrap

to wrap and wrap
and wrap and wrap
in nappies, in singlets
in nighties you wrap
in sheets, in blankets
in shawls you wrap
you wrap and wrap
and wrap and wrap

do the baby rap
do the baby rap
when the grizzly little chappy
calls for his pappy
to clean up his nappy
which is ever so crappy
better do it snappy
if ya wanna keep him happy
do the baby rap
do the baby rap

and when that little bundle
is ready to nap
you rub him and you burp him
and you lie him on your lap

but his feet start to kick
and his arms start to flap
and he goes all red
and his lips start to slap
and you hear that too familiar
rat-tat-tat, tat-tat

o no! the thundering little bundle
has had another crap
and you just know
ya gunna have to unwrap
unwrap, unwrap, unwrap, unwrap
do the baby rap!
■

kompost
kosmos
kosminos
kommodore
komunist
kominios
kominos
fairy floss
kokninos
kondomos
koninios
kondominium
komatozed
kabanosi
kommie snot
komanche
kompact disc
koncord
furry one

a komninos by any other name
would smell ...
the same.

■

don't call me sir

DON'T CALL ME SIR!
MY NAME IS komninos
calling me sir
puts me up
puts you down
i'm the authority
you're the slaves,
or
puts me down
puts you up
here rover
sit down pup.
either way it's not too cool
somebody ends up being somebody's fool.

so
call me komninos
and we'll get on fine
when we're at the same level
our poetry rhymes.
so
if anyone calls me SIR again
i'll let them be mauled by a crazy year ten
or slowly tortured by a terrible year nine
or left to the fate of the whole of year eight
or kissed into heaven by the girls of year seven
and when they're done
to a big year eleven

who'll finally send 'em
to the boys of year seven
who'll cleverly devise
ninety-nine ways
of making you regret your decision
to call me sir
after hearing this poem.
so
please don't call me sir again.
∎

my parents are so daggy that the op shop down the
  road
rings them up to let them know when they throw away
  old clothes.

my father is embarrassing, his taste in cars is yuck
he drops me off to school in a two tonne pickup truck.

my mother's more embarrassing, she's totally uncool
she wants a kiss goodbye, when she drops me off at
   school.

my family is so stingy, there's nothing i can do
they make me pay ten cents just to go to the loo.

my father is so ancient, the oldest man i've ever met,
when he was a boy, he had a dinosaur as a pet.

■

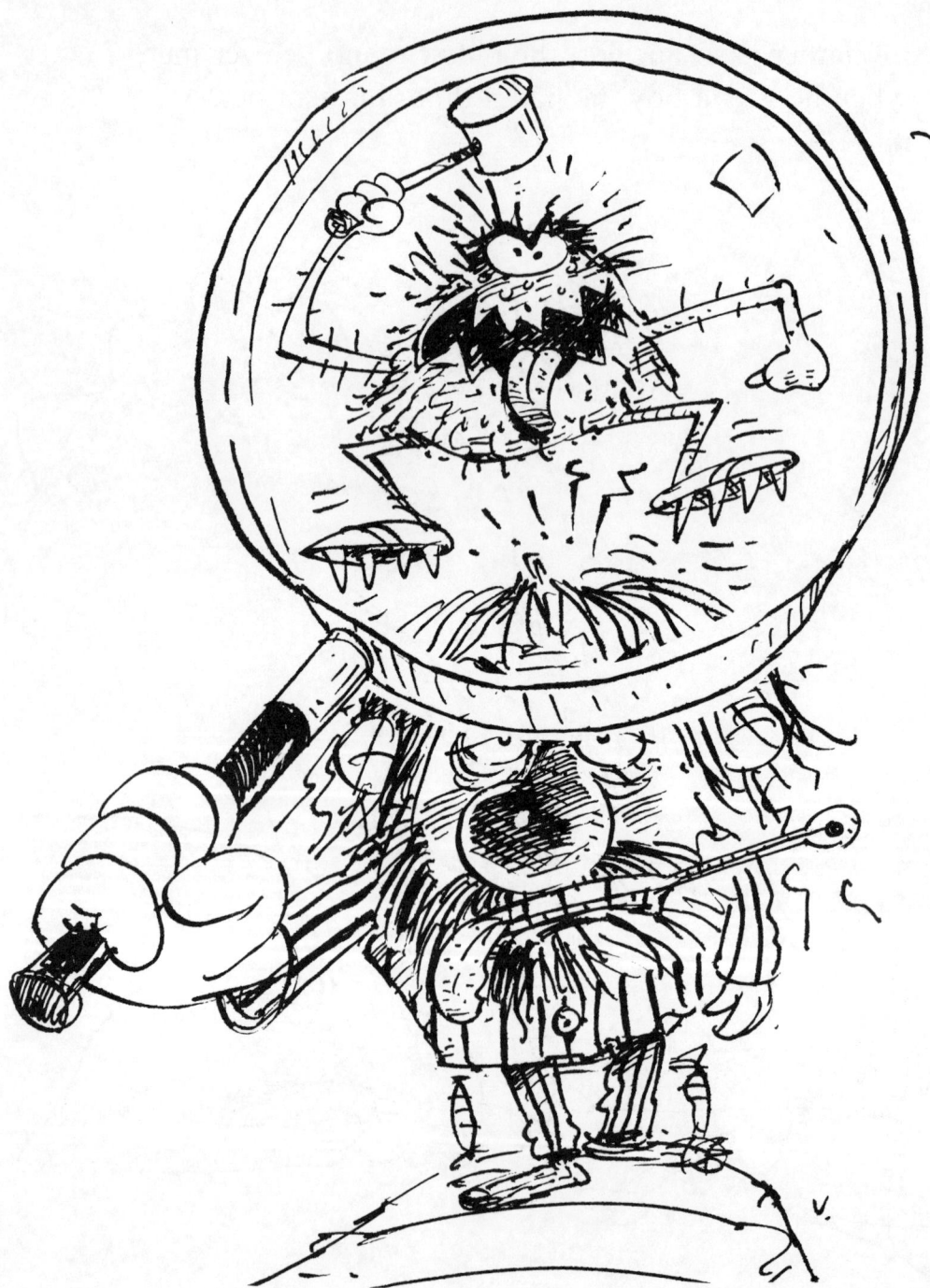

there's a nasty little virus
that's walking round my head
it's pounding across my cranium
in boots all lined with lead.

with spikey-soled running shoes
it races round my nose
it leaves a trail of pricklies
everywhere it goes.

it tickles all my nose hairs
and gives the sneeze button a press
it beats my inner ear drums
my head is in a mess.

the nasty little cold virus
is having so much fun
it turns on all the nose-taps
and lets the mucus run.

a tissue. a tissue. a TISSUE!
my nose wants to explode
it's found the door, it's opened it,
and down my throat it goes.

the virus must be growing fat
it feels just like a frog
each time i open up my mouth
i bark just like a dog.

deep in the darkness of my chest
the virus creeps and crawls
a game of tennis with my lungs
it hits bright green spit balls.

i cough, i wheeze, i feel so weak
this virus has me beat
who'd think something as small as that
could knock me off my feet.

on my muscles it jumps and kicks
it's made them very sore,
'go away you nasty virus
i don't want you any more!'

my stomach hurts, my knees they shake
i feel like being sick.
my tummy's rumbling to my bum
a toilet, a toilet, quick!

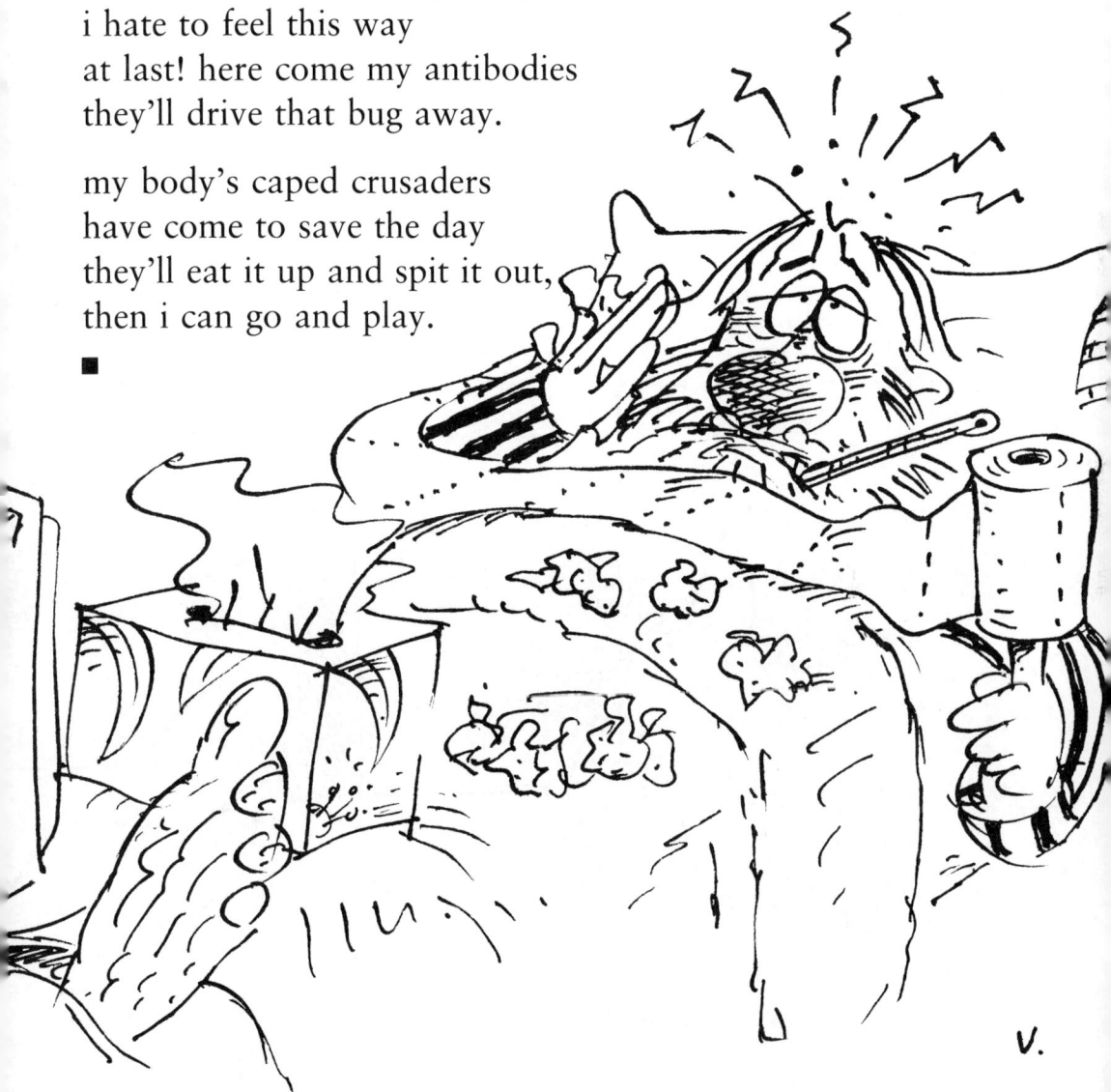

outside my window in the park
i see the children play
whilst in my bed rugged up and warm
yes, that's where i must stay.

o. won't somebody help me please
i hate to feel this way
at last! here come my antibodies
they'll drive that bug away.

my body's caped crusaders
have come to save the day
they'll eat it up and spit it out,
then i can go and play.

■

V.

'jesus saves' the billboard says
two thousand years without a withdrawal
with interest inflation and capital gain
his bank-book must be thicker than the bible
■

when i was young
and had no brains
i ignited crackers
in old storm drains

there was a poor elephant
who had trouble with his bowels
he ate some laxettes
now it's all over town

did you hear about the butcher
who sat on his mincer
his customers complained
he got 'behind' in his orders

we got a dog
we called him brutus because he was strong
when brutus had puppies
we knew we were wrong

why have ducks got big feet?
i heard someone inquire
the answer is quite obvious
to stamp out burning fires!

why have elephants got big feet?
on this question people often get stuck
the answer is also obvious
to stamp out burning ducks

A.A.A. abdul's here today
B.B.B. brett has drawn a tree
C.C.C. christine's writing poetry

D.D.D. danielle has written three
E.E.E. elsa's scratched her knee
F.F.F. fatima's acting deaf
G.G.G. ooh! gail copied me

H.H.H. heidi hates the snakes
I.I.I. ishmail hits the sky
J.J.J. jodie likes to play
K.K.K. kylie's on the way

L.L.L. larry's doing well
M.M.M. mehedin starts again
N.N.N. nicole forgot her pen
O.O.O. orania's on the go

P.P.P. paul wants a wee
Q.Q.Q. that's all we seem to do
R.R.R. rachel likes the caaaaaaaarrs
S.S.S. shaun is in a mess

T.T.T. trong is new to me
U.U.U. ursun's in grade two
V.V.V. vicky's in grade three
W.W.W. walter never troubles you

X.X.X. xeri passed the test
Y.Y.Y. yvette waves me goodbye
Z.Z.Z. zanthi is off to bed

oh. boy.
it's been an extremely alphabetical
            really quite poetical
            definitely multicultural
            very unforgettable,
            day,
            ooh. ray.

                ■

IN THE CITY
CARS WHIZZ BY YOU SO QUICKLY
AND THE TRAFFIC MOVES SO FAST
AND THE TRAMS AND BUSES AND TRUCKS AND
 TRAINS

AND FIRE ENGINES AND TOW TRUCKS AND
STREET SWEEPERS AND GARBAGE TRUCKS
AND AMBULANCES AND HELICOPTERS
AND POLICE CARS AND SIRENS
AND SCREECHING BRAKES
AND BEEPING HORNS
AND MOTOR BIKES

but
in
the
bush
you
can
hear
a
semi
as
it
comes
from
miles
and
miles
away

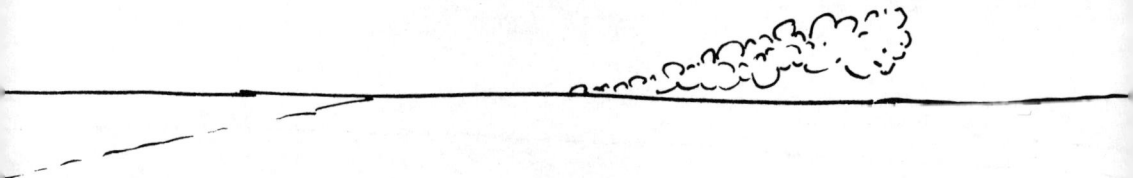

and
as
it
gets
closer
it gets
louder and
louder and
louder and closer
and loudest as it passes

and as it gets further
it gets quieter
and quieter
the further
away
until
you
can
hear
it
less
and
less
un
til
it
fades
in
to
the
night
from
which
it
came ■

it takes a long time
to be a punk.
punks aren't just born.
people with spiked hair
don't just appear out of thin air.
there's lots of
hours
and glue

and gel
and time
and care
and love
that goes into
each and every one
of those spikes. ∎

it's a big city baby
it's getting bigger every day
whichever way you look at it
the city's uncontained
the horror of a hoddle street
queen street jolts the nerves
the rapes, the drugs, the dealers' deaths
the cops, the pimps, the pervs
the cars that kill as fast as guns
as surely as an m-16
the accidents that twist and maim
and shatter lifetime dreams
the cruelty to young people
the indignity to the old
the prizes to the cunning
the callous, the cruel, the cold

46

it's a big city baby
it's getting bigger every day
whichever way you look at it
this city's uncontained
the spread and sprawl of industry
the roads that cut like knives
the buildings that reach high
the wires that trap the sky
the land once wide and sweeping
is divided into blocks
the trees and plants once growing free
now prisoners of pots
the air once fresh and clean
is thick with deadly fumes
and the animals that wandered there
can now be found in zoos

SHOCK
HORROR
DEATH

47

school is so boring, each day it's the same
i do nothing wrong, but i'm always to blame.

school is like a prison, a black dirty hole
twelve years hard labour, without a parole.

school is one big line up, that's all we seem to do
line up for assembly and the classroom too
line up for the canteen, seems all we do is queue.

our school has got a really bad canteen
i once bought a pie that was furry and green.

i get so much homework, much more than anyone
sometimes i pay my sister just to get it done.

video games, at our school, are the big thing
i swapped my skateboard for one that went pinggg!

■

the jarvie park jiggers

jarvie park jiggers really think that they are cool
jigging in the park when they should be back at school.
they gather in the morning underneath the big bay fig
check out their timetables to see when they can jig.

whilst all the other students are assembled in the yard
the jarvie park jiggers are assembled in the park
roula, toula, voula and koula she's there too
ali, smith, nguyen and alexiou
as they all arrive the jiggers roll is marked
the jarvie park jiggers have their roll call in the park.

the year twelve jiggers are the coolest of the cool
sunglasses, styling gel, year twelves rule the school.
watch them rolling up in their cut and polished cars
blow into the park like the marrickville ma-fi-a.

i swear the year elevens are a cunning bunch of jiggers
they sit where they can make their getaway much
  quicker.
hey! look at that rocket up near malakoff
it's filled with so much smoke that i think it's taking
  off.

my god! the year ten jiggers really care about what they
  wear
the boys tease out their egos and the girls tease out their
  hair.

the year nine jiggers hang around so sheepishly
the year eight jiggers just hide behind a tree.
and the year seven jiggers, well i really must be fair
to find a year seven jigger is very, very rare.

you say 'what about the teachers?', there's not a lot that
  they can do
the jarvie park jiggers are a dedicated crew.
they don't do it for kicks, they don't do it for attention
they're so dedicated they give themselves detention
yes, they keep themselves in jarvie park for half an hour
  after school
the way they discipline themselves it really is quite cruel

yes the jarvie park jiggers are a dedicated bunch
the only time they come to school is for recess and for
  lunch
they even come to jarvie park for their school holidays
to pretend that they are jigging, just to pass the time of
  day.

■

ear my class all went on a camp
e teacher in the bushes without a lamp.

we played lots of tricks, and stayed up till four in the
  morning
no wonder the next day we couldn't stop yawning.

the food at the camp was delicious of course
each night spaghetti with rat and maggot sauce.

the weather was great, too good to compare
it didn't stop raining all the time we were there.

the bunks were old, the cabins were damp
the showers were cold, why'd i come on this camp?

■

i hate cats.
well, i mean,
i don't exactly hate them.
but i don't encourage them.

like the other day
grazyna just sat down to eat a bowl of soup.
hubcat jumps up, on the outside window sill.
grazyna,
on the other side,
the inside,
ate her soup.

bright yellow eyes
glanced at grazyna
glanced at the soup
and back to grazyna.
'you're eating, i want some too.'
grazyna was firm.

bright yellow eyes
trying to catch her gaze.
just six inches from the bowl
separated by a window.

eyes
flashing between
the eater
and the soup being eaten.
persistent glances
punctuated by purrs.

i would have given in by then.
the guilt would have killed me.
i'm a sucker for cats,
they walk all over me.
grazyna was firm
she was not going to be guilt-tripped by those
bright yellow eyes.

i hate cats
the way they can guilt trip me like that.

■

laundromat
o laundromat
that is where
it's really at
power wash
and tumble dry
underpants and
socks go by

dirty washing
spinning round
makes a whirring
grinding sound
underwear and
bedsheet smells
o the stories
you could tell

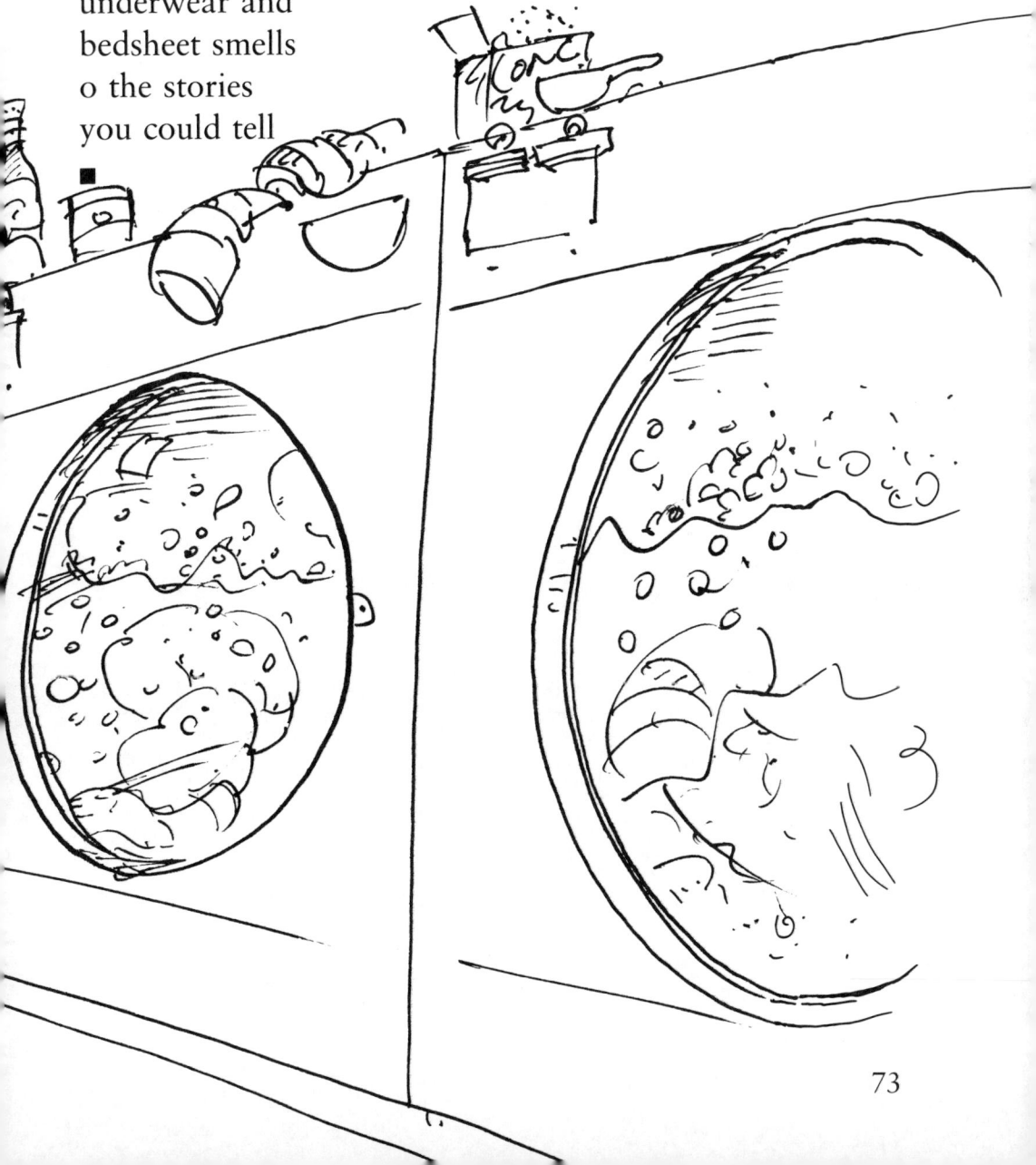

granny's
big pink underpants
is what i think of
when they ask me to go back
to my earliest memories.
me
under her warm black dress
next to her big pink underpants

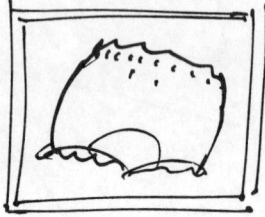

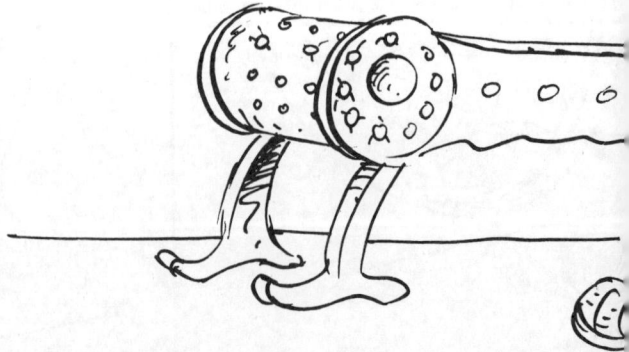

elastic round the edges
left railroads
across her soft white/pink skin
skin
that smelt so sweet
so, so soft to touch
lying for hours
cuddling closely
to granny's
big pink underpants.

■

stove top battlefield
bread crumbs egg and splattered fat
thickly waits a clean.

nestled content'ly
in warm dirt of afternoon
ginger tom cat naps.

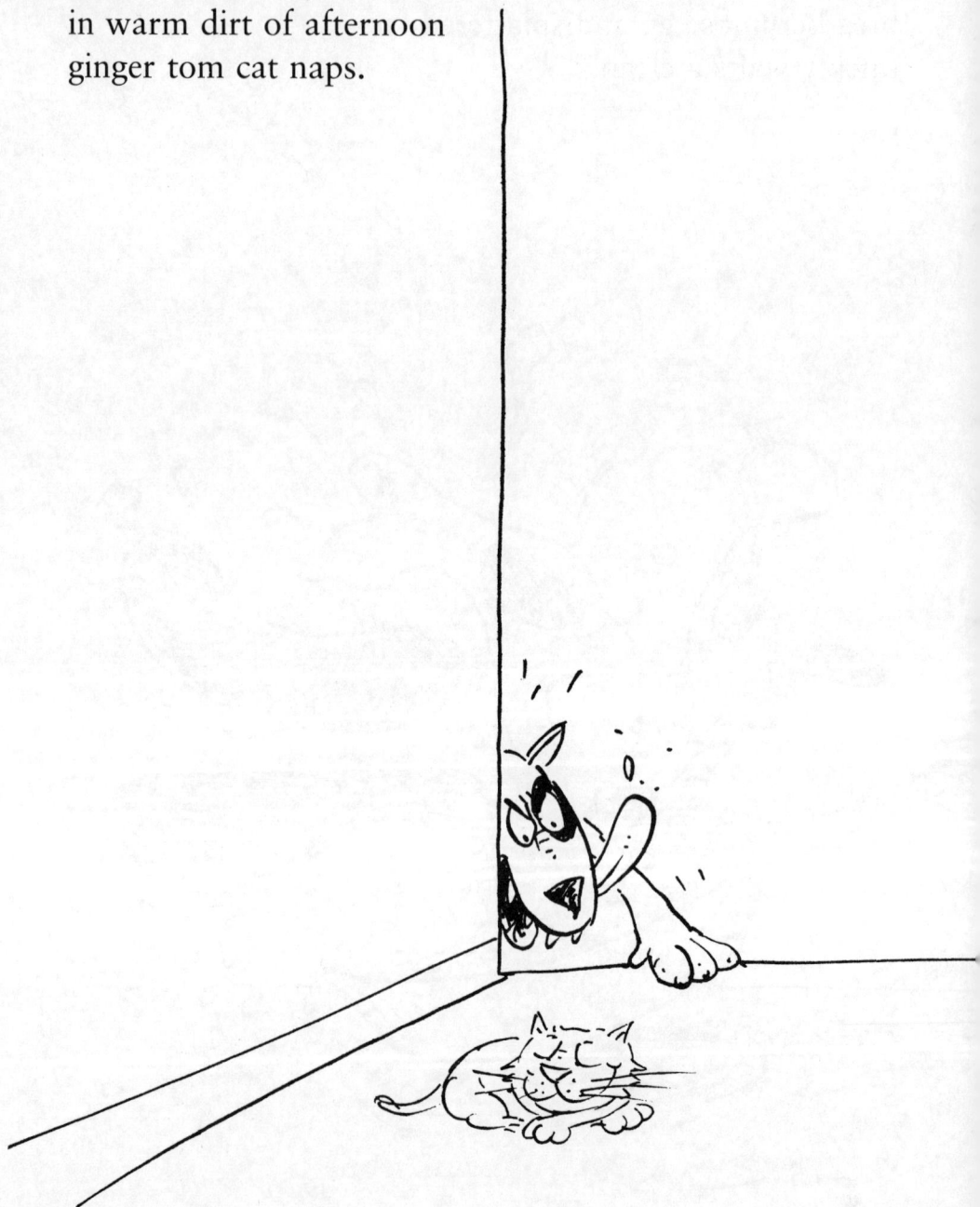

the telephone ringing
renews my relationship
with the outside world.

the traffic noises
wake me announcing the start
of a new work day.

wet shirts on hangers
dance arm in arm on the line
wind gently blowing.

■

i hate
the sound
of drip
ping taps
that drip
and drip
the whole
night through
the drip
is driv
ing me
in sane

that con
stant tap
ping in
my brain
that tap
tap tap
tap tap
tap tap
drip drip
drip drip
drip drip
drip drip

that drip
that drives
me round
the bend
it nev
er nev
er nev
er ends

it drips
all night
and day
time too
there's noth
ing more
that i
can do
to stop
the drip
drip drip
drip drip
how hard
i try
and try
to turn
the knob
and make
it tight
but it
still drips
drip drip
drip drip
all through
the night

drip drip
drip drip

that drip
that hits
on stain
less steel
and pings
and dings
ping ping
ding ding
drip ding
drip ding
tap ping
tap ping
drip ping
drip ping
tap ding
tap ding
bounc ing
off spoons
and forks
and knives
and plates
that need
a wash
ping ping
ding ding
ping ding
ding ping

that drip
that drip
it drips
and drips
un til
i'm real
ly sick
of it
and can
not take
no more
of it
and place
un der
the drip
a sponge
and turn
the ping
in to
a thud
thud thud
thud thud
thud thud
thud thud
■

on the way to the fridge for a snack

fear
comes from
up the hallway when ...
you hear that
creaky noise again.
and no one's home
but yourself and you.

your legs don't move
your senses in tune
and every creak is amplified
and every sound is analysed
your brain, your ears, your nose, your eyes,
are working overtime
what if it's?
or maybe?
it could be.

ohh. what am i going to do?
standing in the same spot all the time
waiting to hear that creak again
waiting for another clue.
ohhh. what am i going to do?
will i go back to my room?
or go down the hall,
and check it out.
maybe it's really nothing at all.
but.
did i turn on the kitchen light?
was that a shadow on the wall?
a shadow that wasn't there before?
what made that flower petal fall?
will i walk down that corridor?
i'll just turn on the hallway light.
but what if it gives
whatever it is, a fright
and it goes off its head
maybe i'll just go to bed.
and hope it goes away.

but
i can't
i couldn't sleep
i have to go and see.
and
with
each
step
i take
the shadows seem
to follow me
my creaky footprints
leave behind
as i go closer all the time
and it's not hot but i start to sweat
the scareder i am the closer i get
and when at last the door i reach
and sigh a welcome sigh of relief
and i shouldn't've been so scared
'cause all the fear was in my head
'cause there was nothing there at all
and i wasn't really scared at all
not much!!!

■

SUPERWOG

look!
up in the sky.
it's a bird.
it's a plane.
no ...
it's SUPERWOG.
strange visitor from a european country
with powers and abilities far beyond those
of normal anglo-saxons.
who can gut and fillet mighty man-eaters,
pick up hot dim-sims in his bare hands.

faster than a squirt of vinegar,
more powerful than tsatsiki,
able to use the lifts in tall buildings.

and who,
disguised as con pappas,
mild mannered fish monger
at a great metropolitan shopping complex

fights a never-ending battle
against mcdonalds,
kentucky fried chicken,
and the american take away.

■
94

i've got the kangaroo blues
i'm a koala munga
but you know i didn't choose
to come down under
'cos i was born in richmond
that's not very far away
i can't go back to where i came from
i guess i'm here to stay.

my mother calls me yiannis
my friends know me as john
don't you think it's funny
they spell my last name wrong
in greece i'm an australian
in australia i'm a greek
i ask myself the question
am i a cultural freak?

on saturday it's football
on sunday it's the soccer
sometimes i don't know at all
if i'm a wog or i'm an ocker
advance advance australia fair
and yia sou re hellenic
i'm a very very funny pair
i'm a cultural schizophrenic.

■

sophisticated souvlaki

from big fat witchety grubs
to salted meat with damper
from fresh fried fish and chips
to take-away hamburger
australia, you've sure made some changes
now there's souvlaki in suburbia

but souvlaki's not the only thing
brought here by the greeks
there's music, dance and poetry
drama, art and politics
souvlaki's just symbolic
of this land's cultural mix

yes australia, we've sure made some changes
but we've still got a long way to go
there has to be more understanding
before we are able to grow

understanding is the basis of acceptance
and acceptance is the basis of peace
we have to have more understanding
no matter what kind of tucker we eat

australia's a cultural smorgasbord
believe what i'm tellin' ya mate
and if you want to be a part of it
get out there and fill up your plate
■

Index of **Titles** and First Lines